D1577459

# GOYA'S *Caprichos*

# GOYA'S
# *Caprichos*

*by* JOSÉ LÓPEZ-REY

# *Beauty, Reason & Caricature*

VOLUME TWO

GREENWOOD PRESS, PUBLISHERS
WESTPORT, CONNECTICUT

*The photographs used for the following illus-
trations are from Más, Barcelona, Spain*

3, 4, 5, 6, 9, 10, 13, 14, 19, 20, 27, 28, 43,
44, 66, 67, 68, 69, 70, 75, 76-84, 89, 91, 93,
95, 97, 103, 104, 108, 110, 111, 113, 118, 123,
125, 128, 132, 135, 139, 141, 143, 146, 150,
153, 156, 158, 163, 166, 168, 170, 172, 173,
175, 177, 179, 181, 183, 185, 187, 188, 190,
192, 194, 196, 198, 200, 203, 205, 207, 211,
213, 215, 217, 223, 232, 234, 235, 238, 240,
241, 243, 245, 247, 249, 254

The original leaf of Figs. 15 and 16 was pur-
chased from the estate of Felix Wildenstein in
November 1952 by the Art Museum of
Princeton University.

# ILLUSTRATIONS

### DRAWINGS FROM THE SANLÚCAR SKETCHBOOK

### DRAWINGS FROM THE MADRID SKETCHBOOK

GOYA'S *Caprichos*

A few of Goya's captions on the margin of the
drawings have been reproduced separately for
greater clarity.

FIG. I

FIG. 2

FIG. 3

FIG. 4

FIG. 5

FIG. 6

FIG. 7

FIG. 8

FIG. 9

FIG. 10

FIG. II

FIG. 12

FIG. 13

FIG. 14

FIG. 15

FIG. 16

FIG. 17

FIG. 18

FIG. 19

FIG. 20

FIG. 21

FIG. 22

FIG. 23

FIG. 24

FIG. 25

FIG. 26

FIG. 27

FIG. 28

FIG. 29

FIG. 30

FIG. 31

FIG. 32

FIG. 33

FIG. 34

FIG. 35

FIG. 36

FIG. 37

FIG. 38

FIG. 39

FIG. 40

El dia de su santo

FIG. 41

FIG. 42

Caricatura alegre

FIG. 43

FIG. 44

masc.

a apunta p.<sup>r</sup> ermofrodita    R.F6914

FIG. 45

FIG. 46

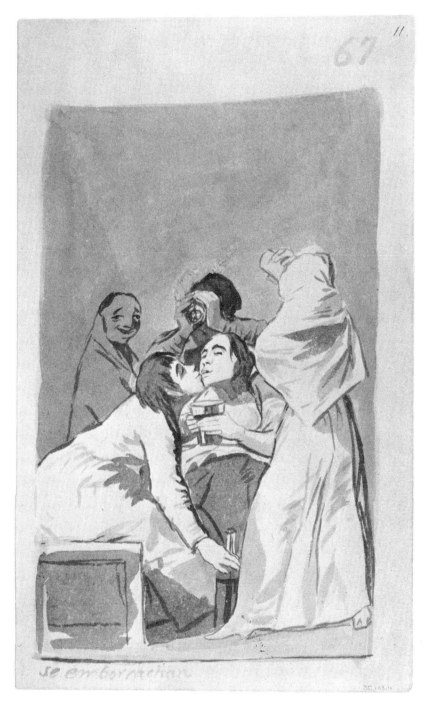

FIG. 47

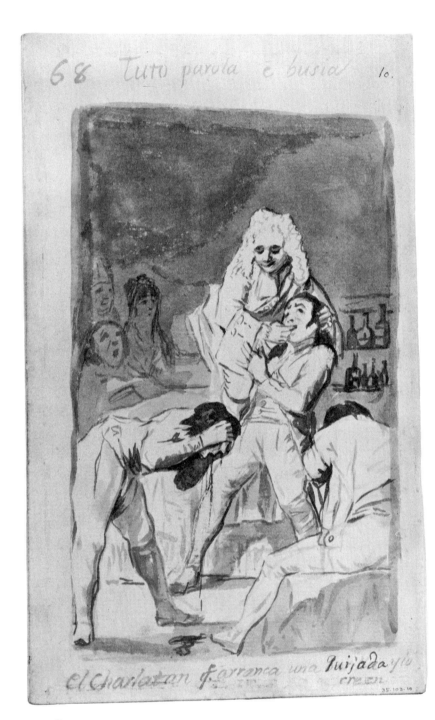

FIG. 48

*Humildad contra soberbia*

FIG. 49

Lardeza contra Abaricia

FIG. 50

Los hermanos de ella, matan a su amante, y ella se mata despues.

FIG. 51

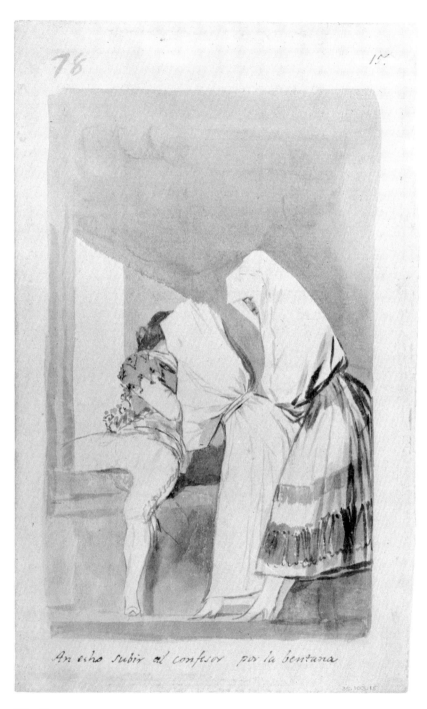

An echo subir al confesor por la bentana

FIG. 52

FIG. 53

Pobres, ¡quantas lo mereceran mejor! ¿pues q.<sup>e</sup> es esto?
que a...... R.l...... las tebana S.<sup>n</sup> fernando.

FIG. 54

Es berano y ala luna, toman el fresco, y se espulgan
al tiento

FIG. 55

Buen Sacerdote ¿donde se ha celebrado?

FIG. 56

*el Abogado.*

*Este a nadie perdona, pero no estan dañino como estar un Medico malo*

FIG. 57

Nobia disreta y arrepentida a ... 
se presenta en esta forma

FIG. 58

FIG. 59

Manda q quiten el coche, se despeina, y
arranca el pelo y patéa

Porq. el abate Pichurris, le á dicho en su ocico, q.
estaba descolorida

FIG. 60

FIG. 61

FIG. 62

2

FIG. 63

FIG. 64

FIG. 65

FIG. 66

FIG. 67

FIG. 68

FIG. 69

FIG. 70

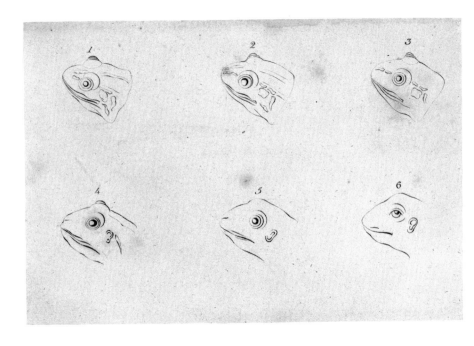

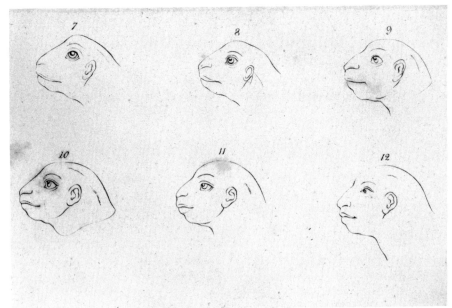

FIG. 71

FIG. 72

FIG. 73

FIG. 74

FIG. 75

39

Vision burlesca

86

FIG. 76

40

Otra en la misma noche

FIG. 77

FIG. 78

FIG. 79

FIG. 80

FIG. 81

FIG. 82

FIG. 83

FIG. 84

FIG. 85

FIG. 86

Fran.co Goya y Lucientes
Pintor.

FIG. 87

El si pronuncian y la mano alargan
Al primero que llega.

FIG. 88

FIG. 89

*Que biene el Coco.*

FIG. 90

FIG. 91

*El de la royona.*

FIG. 92

FIG. 93

*Tal para qual.*

FIG. 94

FIG. 95

*Nadie se conoce.*

FIG. 96

FIG. 97

*Ni asi la distingue.*

FIG. 98

FIG. 99

*Que se la llevaron.*

FIG. 100

FIG. 101

*Tantalo.*

FIG. 102

FIG. 103

FIG. 104

*El amor y la muerte.*

FIG. 105

FIG. 106

*Muchachos al avío.*

FIG. 107

FIG. 108

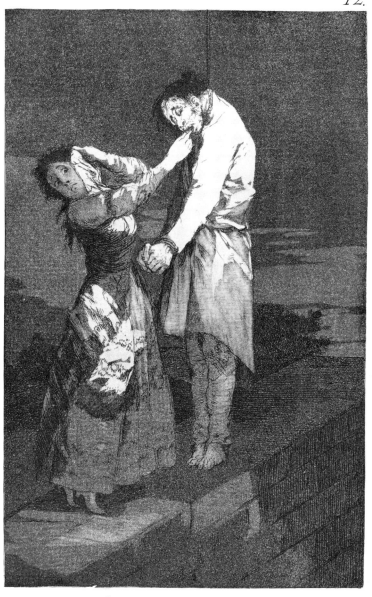

*A caza de dientes.*

FIG. 109

FIG. 110

FIG. III

*Estan calientes.*

FIG. 112

Sacrificio de Ynteres

FIG. 113

*Que sacrificio!*

FIG. 114

*Bellos consejos.*

FIG. 115

FIG. 116

*Dios la perdone: Y era su madre.*

FIG. 117

FIG. 118

*Bien tirada está.*

FIG. 119

FIG. 120

Yse le quema la Casa

FIG. 121

*Ysele quema la Casa).*

FIG. 122

FIG. 123

*Todos Caerán.*

FIG. 124

FIG. 125

FIG. 126

*Ya van desplumados.*

FIG. 127

FIG. 128

¡Qual la descanonan!

FIG. 129

FIG. 130

*Pobrecitas!*

FIG. 131

FIG. 132

*Aquellos polbos.*

FIG. 133

*Nohubo remedio.*

FIG. 134

FIG. 135

*Si quebró el Cantaro.*

FIG. 136

FIG. 137

*Ya tienen asiento.*

FIG. 138

*Antiguo y moderno, Origen del orgullo*

FIG. 139

*Quién mas rendido?*

FIG. 140

FIG. 141

*Chiton.*

FIG. 142

FIG. 143

*Esto si que es leer.*

FIG. 144

FIG. 145

FIG. 146

*Porque esconderlos?*

FIG. 147

13

FIG. 148

*Ruega por ella.*

FIG. 149

FIG. 150

*Por que fue sensible.*

FIG. 151

*Al Conde Palatino.*

FIG. 152

FIG. 153

*Las rinde el Sueño.*

FIG. 154

*Le descañona.*

FIG. 155

FIG. 156

*Mala noche.*

FIG. 157

FIG. 158

*Si sabrá mas el discipulo?*

FIG. 159

FIG. 160

*Brabisimo!*

FIG. 161

FIG. 162

FIG. 163

*Asta su Abuelo.*

FIG. 164

FIG. 165

FIG. 166

*De que mal morira?*

FIG. 167

FIG. 168

*Ni mas ni menos.*

FIG. 169

FIG. 170

*Tu que no puedes.*

FIG. 171

FIG. 172

FIG. 173

El sueño
de la razon
produce
monstruos

FIG. 174

FIG. 175

*Hilan delgado.*

FIG. 176

FIG. 177

*Mucho hay que chupar.*

FIG. 178

FIG. 179

*Correccion.*

FIG. 180

FIG. 181

*Obsequio á el maestro.*

FIG. 182

FIG. 183

*Soplones?*

FIG. 184

FIG. 185

*Duendecitos.*

FIG. 186

La Enfermedad de la Razon

FIG. 187

FIG. 188

Las Chinchillas.

FIG. 189

FIG. 190

*Se repilen.*

FIG. 191

FIG. 192

*Lo que puede un Sastre!*

FIG. 193

FIG. 194

*Que pico de Oro!*

FIG. 195

FIG. 196

*El Vergonzoso.*

FIG. 197

FIG. 198

*Hasta la muerte.*

FIG. 199

FIG. 200

*Subir y bajar.*

FIG. 201

FIG. 202

FIG. 203

La filiacion.

FIG. 204

FIG. 205

*Tragala perro.*

FIG. 206

FIG. 207

*Y aun no se van!*

FIG. 208

FIG. 209

*Ensayos.*

FIG. 210

FIG. 211

*Volaverunt.*

FIG. 212

5

FIG. 213

*Quien lo creyera!*

FIG. 214

FIG. 215

*Miren que grabes!*

FIG. 216

FIG. 217

*Buen Viage*

FIG. 218

Sueño.

Bruja poderosas que por ydropica, sacan a paseo las mejores bolaoras.

FIG. 219

Donde vá mamá?

FIG. 220

Sueño.
Bruja maestra Dando lecciones a su discipulo del primer buelo.

FIG. 221

*Allá vá eso.*

FIG. 222

FIG. 223

*Aguarda que te unten).*

FIG. 224

FIG. 225

*Linda maestra!*

FIG. 226

FIG. 227

*Sopla.*

FIG. 228

FIG. 229

FIG. 230

*Devota profesion.*

FIG. 231

FIG. 232

*Si amanece ; nos Vamos.*

FIG. 233

FIG. 234

FIG. 235

No te escaparás

FIG. 236

*Mejor es holgàr.*

FIG. 237

FIG. 238

*No grites, tonta.*

FIG. 239

FIG. 240

FIG. 241

*¿No hay quien nos desate?*

FIG. 242

FIG. 243

¿Està Vm.d pues, Como digo.. eh¡Cuidado¡si nó..

FIG. 244

FIG. 245

*Unos à otros.*

FIG. 246

FIG. 247

*Despacha, que dispiertan.*

FIG. 248

FIG. 249

*Nadie nos ha visto.*

FIG. 250

*Ya es hora.*

FIG. 251

FIG. 252

FIG. 253

FIG. 254

FIG. 255

FIG. 256

Tab. XVII.1.

FIG. 257

FIG. 258

FIG. 259

FIG. 260

FIG. 261

FIG. 262

FIG. 263

Peint au Pastel par Ch. Coypel.                                    Gravé par L. Surugue en 1745.

La Folie pare la Décrépitude des ajustemens
de la Jeunesse.

a Paris chez L. Surugue Graveur du Roy rue des Noyers, attenant le Magazin de Papier vis-a-vis S.t Yves. A.P.D.R.

FIG. 264

FIG. 265